The Workbook

Proper Care & Management of Your Geeks
by Dennis Aramanda, copyright 2020

The Workbook, Proper Care and Management of Your Geeks

Copyright © 6-4-2020 by Dennis Aramanda All rights reserved. No part of this publication may be reproduced, distributed, or transmitted in any form or by any means, including photocopying, recording, or other electronic or mechanical methods, without the prior written permission of the publisher, except in the case of brief quotations embodied in critical reviews and certain other noncommercial uses permitted by copyright law. For permission requests, send email to the publisher, addressed "Attention: Permissions Coordinator," at the email address below.
Please send requests or questions to Dennis@HelpingYourGeeks.com
First Edition

The Workbook, Proper Care and Management of Your Geeks

Contents

Chapter 1   Who, what, and why the book? 5
Chapter 2   About Geeks 7
    Geeks have feelings too. 8
    Geeks motivations 8
    How to use the motivations to get work done. 9
    Motivation Exercise 10
Chapter 3   Getting to know your Geeks. 11
    Sincerity and Honesty are keys 12
    Geeks normally do not need a big group of friends. 12
    Geeks have a hard time trusting. 12
    Hobbies 13
    Family Life 13
Chapter 4   Geek Speak (aka Communication with Geeks 101) 15
    How to talk with Geeks 16
    How to have discussions and keep emotions separated. 16
    Think before you speak. 16
    Only ask if you are willing to listen (for real). 17
    Questions to ask that are allowed 17
    Good questions to ask Geeks: 17
    Be honest 18
    How to listen to Geeks 18
    Prepare to Listen. 18
    Do not interrupt to correct. 18
    Follow-up is _____ 18
  What to do if you made a mistake. 19
    Error in information 19
    Personal / Hurt Feelings 19
Chapter 5   Managing Geeks 20
    A Strategy that works for groups and individuals. 21
    Future Goals (1- and 5-year outlooks) 22
    Attainable Objectives / Year Goals 22
    A Clear Purpose Must Exist 23
    Boundary Setting 23

For free tools go to   HelpingYourGeeks.com

- Clear rules 23
- Clear consequences 23
- Ways to have discussions (Rules of engagement.) 23
- If it sounds like arguing, and looks like arguing...is it arguing? 23
- Mentoring Geeks 24
- Clear the road for your Geeks 24

Chapter 6 Growing Geeks 25
- Growth Plan 26
- Geek Training 27
- Challenges are good 27
- Provide Direction 27
- Group Training when needed. 27
- Better Communications for Geeks and Beyond 27
- Using Conferences to learn 28

Chapter 7 Protect your Geeks 29
- Standing up for your Geeks. 30
- Standing with your Geeks 30
- Do what you can, when you can. 31
- Team Building 31
- Loyalty is hard to gain, but is priceless when attained. 31

Chapter 8 Problemed Geeks 32
- The know it all Geek 33
- Geeks without Goals 33
- Hurtful and Helpful Geeks 33
- Geek Promotions 35

Conclusion 37

Chapter 1 Who, what, and why the book?

The Workbook, Proper Care and Management of Your Geeks

Geeks Defined:
_____
_____
_____
_____

This training is based on more than __ years of proven experience.

Experiences from both being a geek and leading geeks as a manager in a Fortune _____ 100 company.

The purpose of this book is to both _____ the leadership in companies to better understand their geeks, as well as help the geeks be able to _____ and _____ personally. This will help both to _____ in the future.

Management often makes the mistake in believing that the end product from the Geeks is the most critical component for the company's success.

Note Space: _____
_____
_____
_____
_____
_____
_____
_____
_____
_____
_____
_____
_____
_____
_____
_____
_____

Chapter 2   About Geeks

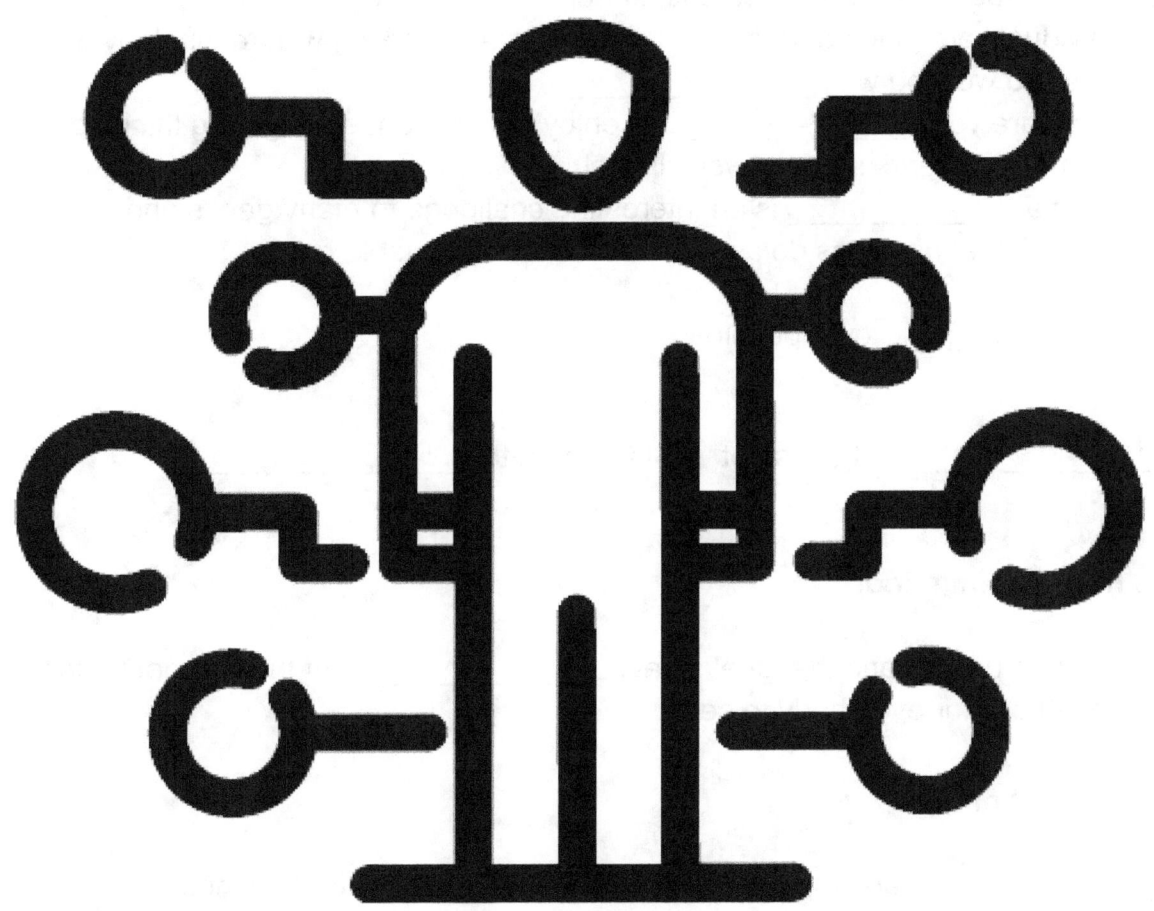

The Workbook, Proper Care and Management of Your Geeks

First let me say Geek is not a derogatory term but rather an accepted descriptor for those who design, program, test and support technology, more specifically software.

Technology Geeks have developed into a unique group that exists in today's workplace more prevalently than ever before.

As we have moved from a _____ economy to a _____ economy this group has differentiated itself from the worker of the past.
These individuals are gifted and talented more towards working with technology and possibly less so working with _____.
Usually, they are very _____-_____ and enjoy the challenge of figuring things out that are on the more esoteric or non-physical level.
Thinking like a _____ is an interesting challenge to many geeks and being able to make these machines do as they wish is an acceptable goal.

They tend to like _____ over people.

Like _____ but does not want to be on the _____.

Geeks have feelings too.

It's important to understand that geeks have _____, but they do not usually express emotions for everybody to see.

Geeks motivations

_____ are important. They're the reason people do things.

There may be _____ times of the year that time off is more important to the geek (where they have more time off), or money is important (maybe it's getting close to Christmas and they want to have more funds for presents or something of that nature), or they need their flexibility in their schedule and that becomes a motivation for them.

So, keeping up with their _____ and realizing that they do change is important.

Geeks' _____ usually are not as straightforward as "They are just working for money."

How to use the motivations to get work done.

Managers can use this information to best keep their geeks motivated, on task, and accomplishing the company's goals.

It is a misnomer to think that geeks can be motivated to accomplish something _____.

Note Space: _____
_____
_____
_____
_____
_____
_____
_____
_____
_____
_____
_____
_____
_____
_____
_____
_____
_____
_____
_____
_____
_____
_____
_____
_____
_____

For free tools go to   HelpingYourGeeks.com

The Workbook, Proper Care and Management of Your Geeks

Here is a motivation tool that may help in finding out what best motivates an individual.

Motivation Exercise

List the following from 1 to 22 in the order that is Most important to you and that will motivate you the most to perform your best every day at your job.

ACHIEVEMENT	MORE MONEY
ADVANCEMENT	OPPORTUNITY
CHALLENGE	POWER
COMPETITION	RECOGNITION
CONGRATULATIONS	RELATIONSHIP WITH BOSS
CREATIVITY	RELATIONSHIP WITH PEERS
ENTHUSIASTIC BOSS	RESPONSIBILITY
FLEXIBLE HOURS	THANK YOU
GOALS / OBJECTIVES	TIME OFF
JOB SECURITY	WORK ITSELF
MONEY	WORKING CONDITIONS

Note: A reminder about trust, Do NOT share the resulting information without absolute expressed permission of the one who filled in their results.

The best way to use these Motivation results is by focusing on those areas of highest priority for each individual. The amount and how may be a discussion between the manager and HR as to what is acceptable.

1		12	
2		13	
3		14	
4		15	
5		16	
6		17	
7		18	
8		19	
9		20	
10		21	
11		22	

Chapter 3   Getting to know your Geeks.

The Workbook, Proper Care and Management of Your Geeks

When I first realized that part of working professionally was to get to know the people that I work with and build a relationship with them, I had a rough time. At that point I was contracting and I felt if I were not _____ then I was _____ time which was not what I wanted. It took a while for me to do a couple of important things to help with this realization. The first of which is to be _____ when talking with people; from the perspective of something as simple as, 'How are you doing?' and really meaning it. When they responded, I'd ask them pertinent questions based on their _____.

Sincerity and Honesty are keys

_____ and _____ are keys to getting to know your Geeks deeper. Geeks will usually only open up to those they _____ really care.

_____ is just being always truthful with others. Geeks are very good at sensing dis_____.

Geeks normally do not need a big group of friends.

Popularity is not a key driver for Geeks. Although we all enjoy acceptance, they tend to have a smaller circle of _____, but that's their preference.

The word "_____" is not taken lightly, and so, does not translate to acquaintance (the more recent definition), chum, buddy, mate, confidante, or comrade. The tendency is to be very precise to the meaning of the word, such as from UrbanDictionary.com:
"A friend is someone you love and who loves you, someone you respect and who respects you, someone whom you trust and who trusts you. A friend is honest and makes you want to be honest, too. A friend is loyal."
Understand that your goal is to work better with and manage Geeks, not to befriend all of them. You do not have to be considered a _____ in order to be accepted as a great Manager.

Geeks have a hard time trusting.

They have a hard time trusting _____. When it comes to working for a company, it takes time for them to trust who they work for. Please note that the trust is in _____ they report to or work for, not the _____.

For free tools go to   HelpingYourGeeks.com

# The Workbook, Proper Care and Management of Your Geeks

The best way to get to know them is by talking to them as _____ and realizing that it's going to take time (Patience).

If there will be a change in Management, it is critical for the new _____ to understand how to build relationships, and not to expect that the respect and loyalty from the Geeks has anything to do with _____.

Hobbies

Geeks usually have hobbies that are _____ and/or detailed in nature, not necessarily _____.

Some examples:
_____
_____
_____

Family Life

The family life of Geeks is very _____, and therefore not usually talked about to strangers.
Talking about family is kept to a minimal level since the normal belief is that people speak _____ and do not really _____.

If Geeks do not see any sincerity in the person talking with them, their level of _____ goes down since they see no reason or benefit to truly share; why waste their time?

The Workbook, Proper Care and Management of Your Geeks

_____ is important and very integral to trust.

Anything spoken of, that does not have to do directly with work, is being told in _____.

If you feel a need to share information unrelated to work with others, attain _____ FIRST.

Asking forgiveness in this area will lose _____ instantly. Be respectful of their wishes in response to you obtaining permission. _____ means no.

If you ever feel that something being said to you is uncomfortable or inappropriate, _____ the conversation and state your concerns.

Note Space: _____
_____
_____
_____
_____
_____
_____
_____
_____
_____
_____
_____
_____
_____
_____
_____
_____
_____
_____
_____
_____
_____
_____
_____

For free tools go to   HelpingYourGeeks.com

Chapter 4   Geek Speak (aka Communication with Geeks 101)

How to talk with Geeks

A good way to start certain kinds of conversations, training, or discussions is to actually start off by saying that you realize that you do not _____ what they do or do not know. You can ask what they may _____, or _____ ahead of time that if they feel like they're being spoken down to or anything of that nature they can let you know.

They don't have to _____ to listen because you are their boss, you are asking for collaboration.

How to have discussions and keep emotions separated.

One thing to learn as a manager is how to have discussions and keep emotion separated. Understand when discussing work that's been performed, geeks may take any kind of criticism of their _____ personally as opposed to keeping it separate.
So, it's difficult at times to tell _____ that something didn't work correctly without them hearing that _____ are not working correctly.

What this means is that you have to come up with ways to discuss work that's been performed in a way that _____ understand that you're talking about the product or work that was done, as opposed to them personally.

Think before you speak.

This is _____, simple, but _____. As we said earlier Geeks take words to be very meaningful and specific. Most have a very large vocabulary and deliberate internally before speaking. The more knowledgeable they are in an area, the more _____ they are in talking.

It gets geeks frustrated when people use words _____.
So, when you speak with geeks take the time needed to formulate your thoughts and express them with words that are appropriate and concise to relay your meaning.

The Workbook, Proper Care and Management of Your Geeks

While there are many people that nod their heads and allow a conversation to continue, _____ are more likely to bring it to a halt. One reason for this would be to request clarification on something that has been said. Another reason may be to interject some knowledge that they feel would benefit everyone. They do not usually know that it is _____, but rather that the interruption needs to take place for better understanding before the conversation proceeds.

Only ask if you are willing to listen (for real).

Only ask questions if you're willing to _____ and _____ the answer.
Be prepared to receive questions in response.

Questions to ask that are allowed.

There is a prevalent saying that exists, "There is no such thing as a dumb, stupid, or bad question."
This idea is _____ shared by Geeks.

Good questions to ask Geeks:

- Things directly from _____ topic; Ask about more in-depth details of a specific point that was mentioned.

- _____ of what has been stated.

- Direct questions regarding things _____ but not the geek themselves.
    Be careful that questions do not have or use the words "_____" or "_____", unless there is a needed intent to ask something about the Geek.

Be honest

When interacting with Geeks, be _____. In general.

Being honest includes telling complete truths. _____ truths can be just as damaging as _____ and both are considered dishonest by Geeks.

When interacting with geeks, do not attempt to _____ to _____ things being stated. It is accepted that not everyone knows everything. Being forward about not knowing or not fully understanding something is usually taken as being a good person and helps in building trust.

How to listen to Geeks

Prepare to Listen.

Stop what you are doing and provide full _____ to the person speaking to you. Everyone likes to know they are being heard. Do not check your _____ or your _____ put your _____ down. If a call or text comes in that can wait, let it go to voicemail or ignore it.

Do not interrupt to correct.

Interrupting a flow of thought being shared with correction that is _____ really pertinent to what is understood and being communicated may only impede the knowledge share taking place.

Taking _____ is OK

While the geek is speaking, take notes about what is being said (do not make a grocery list). If in a one-on-one conversation, let the other person know upfront that you may take notes. When taking notes gather questions or concerns for when it is your turn to speak.

Follow-up is _____
Sometimes you will not have the answers immediately for your Geeks. Let them know you will investigate and get back to them. Providing a timeline, when possible, (in two days, a week, etc...) will reassure them of your sincerity. _____ get back within the time limit provided, or request more time, if needed. Missing the timeline is _____ to the relationship and will cause a loss in trust.

What to do if you made a mistake.

_____
_____
_____

Error in information

_____
_____
_____

Personal / Hurt Feelings

The following is not to be done lightly. If not meant, then do not bother wasting time or effort to fix this kind of mistake.

_____
_____
_____

Note Space: _____
_____
_____
_____
_____
_____
_____
_____
_____
_____
_____
_____
_____
_____
_____
_____
_____
_____
_____

The Workbook, Proper Care and Management of Your Geeks

Chapter 5   Managing Geeks

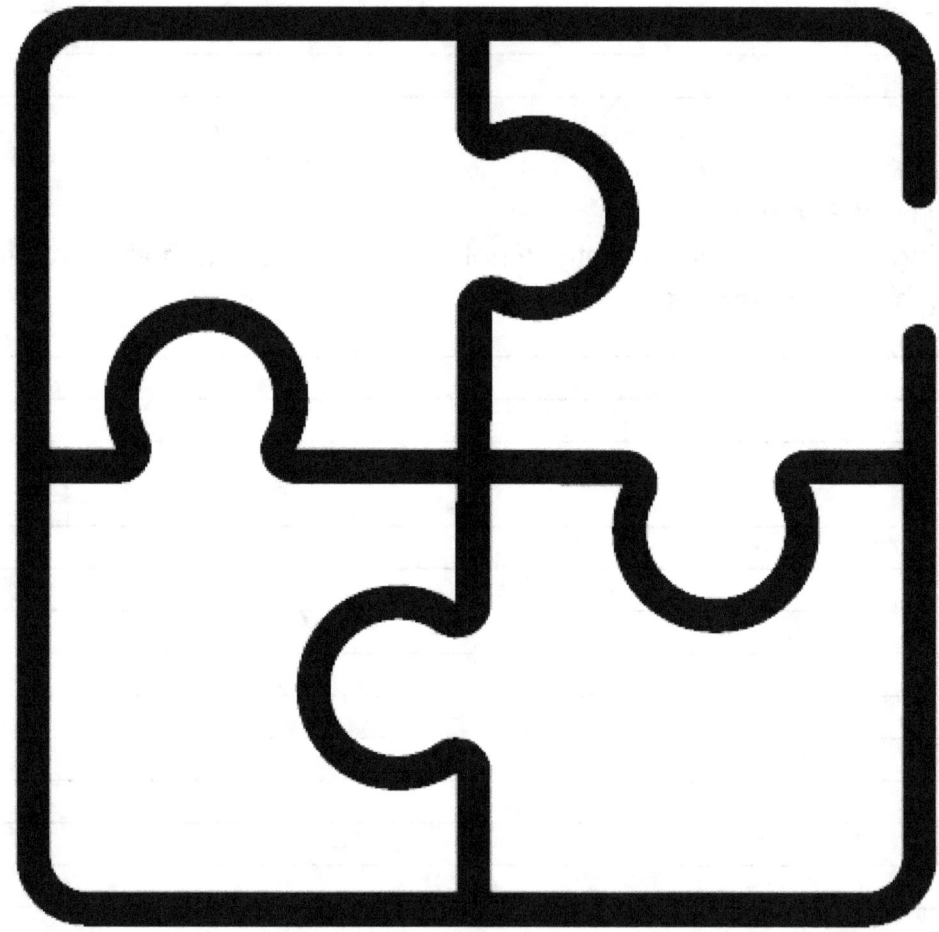

For free tools go to   HelpingYourGeeks.com

A Strategy that works for groups and individuals.

In order to manage Geeks, you need a strategy that works for them in a _____ setting as well as individuals.

Unfortunately, general ways to manage a group D_____ N_____ usually work very well with a group of Geeks.
This is because Geeks do not normally play well together.

For team building you have to come up with a common ground that allows _____ to work together.

The best individual strategy for managing Geeks is to have complete job _____. This allows for expectations to be clearly stated.
This is also key for assigning _____. The reason for this is because they will sometimes over think things and never finish a project because they keep finding more to be done.

You may have to help them to understand _____ limits for accomplishing tasks, and what to do when those limits are reached. Also make it known that the limits are in place for the company's sake and not being used as some kind of negative enforcement of anyone's inability to get something accomplished.

There is such a thing as good enough, and that does not mean _____, just not "perfect".
Having specific goals and time limits will help them to get things done more consistently for what's needed. This will also help in developing a growth plan and can help set future goals for your geeks within the company.

Future Goals (1- and 5-year outlooks)

Help your geeks set goals within the company that allows them success and accountability.
The following is often a tool used in determining if a goal is viable.
SMART is a mnemonic/acronym, giving criteria to guide in the setting of objectives, for example in project management, employee-performance management and personal development.

Attainable Objectives / Year Goals

Letter	Major Term	Minor Terms
S	Specific	Significant, Stretching, Simple
M	Measurable	Meaningful, Motivational, Manageable
A	Attainable	Appropriate, Achievable, Agreed, Assignable, Actionable, Ambitious, Aligned, Aspirational, Acceptable, Action-focused
R	Relevant	Results-oriented, Realistic, Resourced, Resonant
T	Timely	Time-oriented, Time framed, Timed, Time-based, Time boxed, Time-bound, Time-Specific, Timetabled, Time limited, Trackable, Tangible

(Five-year plan, help your geek imagine where they may be in future. This should be reviewed at least once a year with revision as needed.)

A Clear Purpose Must Exist

Any Geek should be able to explain what their _____ is within the company. If this is not true, then it is management's job to clarify. Geeks should also have an idea of how they are working towards accomplishing their goals.

The key here is to be sure that the _____ component is explicit enough that the Geek will know how and what to provide to fulfill it. An example of this would be that if the goal is for the Geek to attend three training sessions during the year, then the Measurable component could be that the Geek will provide _____ showing they attended.

Boundary Setting
Clear rules

Geeks need clear _____ to work by. Spell out boundaries that exist from financial, time, and even Human Resources. Some Geeks like to push limits, just to see how far things may be taken. If the _____ are set and _____, they will be taken more seriously.

Clear consequences

These rules should also have clear _____. Whenever possible list the consequences for breaking rules.

Explain, with examples, of what may happen or has happened in the past. Be ready to allow consequences to take place. When geeks break rules, they need to know that it is not acceptable and receive their due result.

Ways to have discussions (Rules of engagement.)

- Discussion
- Arguing
- Location (where loud discussions can be ok)
- Unacceptable methods of communication
- Who is the moderator and able to control and / or shut-down the discussion

If it sounds like arguing, and looks like arguing...is it arguing?
One thing to keep in mind is that it's common for geeks' discussions to become intense because of their strong beliefs, strong opinions, and emotions. That is why having rules will help. It will provide guidelines for all to follow and help to set expectations of control to be maintained.

Mentoring Geeks

_____ must exist, or Mentoring WILL _____ take place.

Just because individuals meet and talk about one of their jobs, it is not enough to be called Mentoring. Attempting to forcibly Mentor someone is more likely Coaching. Giving advice for growth should only be provided to geeks when trust already exists.

Clear the road for your Geeks

How do they get
- needed information
- tools
- software
- permissions
-

Note Space: _____

_____
_____
_____
_____
_____
_____
_____
_____
_____
_____
_____
_____
_____
_____
_____
_____
_____
_____
_____
_____
_____

Chapter 6   Growing Geeks

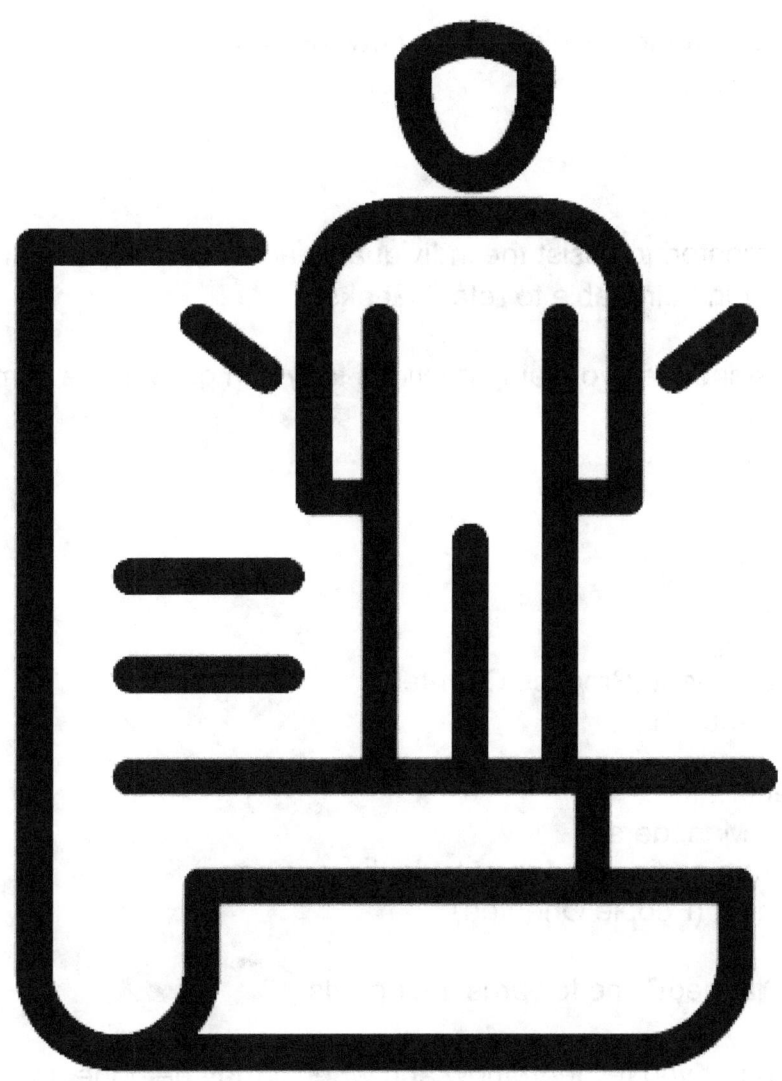

Growth Plan
The Geek should know where they are within the company's organizational structure, and how they have the opportunity to grow.

Help document a plan with the geek to show how they can grow.
Primary areas to grow are:
- Monetarily
- Educationally
- Positionally

Having a plan documented to assist the individual in accomplishing the above growth areas is a Key Factor in being able to retain Geeks.

Help them to understand the two main directions they can go within a company
- technology path
- management path.

Technology Path
- Certifications
- Software training
- Project Management (Process Oriented)
- Agile - Scrum Master

People Management Path
- Education for Managers
- Leadership training (inside and outside the company)
- Project Planning (People Oriented)

Ensure they have Planned Time towards their goals.

If they cannot tell you or you tell them how and when it may be done, then it will not happen.

Why in time will this count against the company?
_____
_____
_____

How can you help your geeks keep ownership and stay on track of their goals?

_____
_____
_____

Worth noting is that not all geeks are looking to advance. They are comfortable staying on top of their current skills and keeping in their current position. If that supports the company's goals, then that should be supported.

Geek Training
Challenges are good
Many Geeks do not like infinite, consistent _____.

Learn the limits of your geeks regarding _____. Too much will cause mental overload and STUCK thinking.

To resolve mental overload and STUCK thinking either control the number of _____ being given or teach them how to break down tasks into smaller, more manageable chunks. Though this may seem counterintuitive, sometimes knowing the _____ _____ may not be a good thing.

Provide Direction
_____
_____
_____
_____
_____

Group Training when needed.
If there are new processes or software that everyone must learn, think about making it group training.
- Have a consultant come into the company and let them teach
- Lunch and Learns

Better Communications for Geeks and Beyond

Geeks can be very interesting to work with in the area of Communication. They are the only group I have worked with over the past 30 years that consistently will say they are great at communicating but usually are not.
- DISC Personality Assessment
- Getting to know others/the team

The best way to sell this to Geeks is to point out that regardless of what they do, they will have to work with other people, so why not make things easier on themselves.

For a company, it would be worthwhile to provide some kind of reward or special incentive if they complete and provide real feedback, or knowledge via open discussion.

Get permission for this to occur on company time (in the long run the company will benefit the most anyway).

Using Conferences to learn

- Make sure geeks have turned in an Itinerary of what they plan to do while at the conference.
- Get a written report after they return.
- Have them share with the team the things they learned.
- Ensure that they understand the company's policy on continued education with reimbursement.

Note Space: _____
_____
_____
_____
_____
_____
_____
_____
_____
_____
_____
_____
_____
_____
_____
_____
_____
_____
_____

Chapter 7   Protect your Geeks

First, as their manager, you are responsible to the company for everything your geeks are doing. When things go wrong due to mistakes you will be the first one called. This includes when they have issues based on responses they provide in person or via email.

- They have a responsibility to you for what they do.
- Pay attention when told of their external interactions.
- The key is to have enough trust and respect that they will tell you before you have to ask them.
- Things do not happen out of the clear blue, if looked at in hindsight. Clues of difficulty within or outside groups will exist.

Standing up for your Geeks.

Be prepared to deal with other parts of the company regarding your Geeks. They need to know that you have their back. That you watch out for their best interests.
Be sure your Geeks know what you will and will not do for them.
Having this kind of understanding makes for a much happier working team.
Some examples

_____
_____
_____
_____
_____

What to do if you overhear comments about a team member being made fun of.
_____
_____
_____

Standing with your Geeks
During difficult work tasks / Emergencies

You may not be able to contribute directly, your team needs to know you are with them.
- Perhaps be on a call just listening.
- Even if the geeks do not tell you it is important to them, even if they outwardly say that you may leave, do not.
- Others are always watching and paying attention.
- There may be a time that you can make a difference by being involved.

- By doing this, you show them you are there with them, after all you are responsible.
- Set a plan of action, with time limits. Sometimes someone just has to make the call that the Back Out is required.

Do what you can, when you can.
- Investigate/research if you can help.
- Offer to take notes
- Keep other groups apprised with periodic updates

Team Building
Take everyone to lunch when allowed. Can go a long way and provide a great chance to hear what is going on, beyond the traditional meeting.

Loyalty is hard to gain, but is priceless when attained.
Loyalty attainment goes beyond trust.
What it is
_____
_____
_____

How to help it exist
_____
_____
_____

Signs that help you know it exists
_____
_____
_____

Be careful what you say about other teams and their leadership. Your team will pick up on it and may take things further than you would ever want them to go.

Note Space: _____
_____
_____
_____
_____

The Workbook, Proper Care and Management of Your Geeks

Chapter 8   Problemed Geeks

Like any employee there are some geeks that require even more special attention. The key is to not discount the positive because of the negative, and maximize the value for your company.

The know it all Geek
How to identify when someone is acting like one
_____
_____
_____

The main problem
_____
_____
_____

Geeks without Goals
How to identify when someone is acting like one
_____
_____
_____

The main problem
_____
_____
_____

Hurtful and Helpful Geeks

Geeks that think they are helping, but are actually NOT sometimes do not realize they are being hurtful, so a quick side talk may be needed to let them know.
How this most often happens
_____
_____
_____

The Workbook, Proper Care and Management of Your Geeks

Scenario / Example
_____
_____
_____
_____
_____
_____
_____

Note Space: _____
_____
_____
_____
_____
_____
_____
_____
_____
_____
_____
_____
_____
_____
_____
_____
_____
_____
_____
_____
_____
_____
_____

Geek Promotions
Realize the value of these "individual contributors"

Geeks being promoted commonly have two paths.

The Technology Path
_____
_____
_____

The People Management Path
_____
_____
_____

Since Career Paths are normally split between Job Grades and Salary Bands, I will leave you to work with your Human Resource department to understand those details and how they work in your company.
Notes
_____
_____
_____

Here are key areas to be sure and make a file on and keep available –

- Know what positions exist for your Geeks moving into the future.
- Document what requirements are needed to attain these positions.
- Document how to get the requirements accomplished.

Geeks do _____ when involved with where they are going in the future of the company.
Geeks do _____ when pushed into the future.

Be very mindful when wanting to promote a geek into a position that has them leading others. They most often will accept any promotion without hesitation, even if it _____ them and they do not want anything to do with it.
Many a well intending manager has taken a geek who is fantastic at their job, promoted them into a leadership role only to have them become _____ over time and eventually _____.

If the goal is to just get them a raise, figure out another way. Leadership is not for everyone and everyone does not want to be in leadership. Giving a geek a leadership position just because it is the only way the company will allow them to get a raise potentially sets the geek up to be "let go" later because they are not "doing" the tasks of the role, the one that they were given to give them a pay increase NOT new / different things to "do" in the first place.

There are a lot of geeks that don't want to go into _____, they truly enjoy what they're doing and want to stay there.

Note Space: _____
_____
_____
_____
_____
_____
_____
_____
_____
_____
_____
_____
_____
_____
_____
_____
_____
_____
_____
_____
_____
_____
_____
_____
_____
_____
_____
_____

Conclusion

The number of geeks and their importance in the workforce is only growing, but sadly understanding of how to help this special section of employees has not. You may get a feeling from the beginning of the book that relationships (or people in general) are not all that important to this group of folks. Hopefully this training has been a help and you found just the opposite to be true.

The idea that "Helping your geeks 'might' help your company", may be better re-stated as, "Helping your geeks 'has' the potential to save your company and propel it to an entire new level!"

If you feel this makes sense and you are interested in what we are sharing in order to help you help your geeks then contact us at HelpingYourGeeks.com to schedule a call to see how we can help you and your company today!

On-Site Conferences to train managers
On-Site Conferences to build up and encourage your geeks
Consulting services and much, much more!

HelpingYourGeeks.com